SpiritGifts

PARTICIPANT'S WORKBOOK

This workbook belongs to

_____

SpiritGifts

PARTICIPANT'S WORKBOOK

PATRICIA D. BROWN

Abingdon Press
Nashville

SPIRITGIFTS: PARTICIPANT'S WORKBOOK

Copyright © 1996 by Abingdon Press

This book is printed on acid-free, recycled paper.

ISBN 0-687-00858-1

Scripture quotations are from the New Revised Standard Version Bible, copyright © 1989, by the Division of Christian Education of the National Council of the Churches of Christ in the United States of America. Used by permission.

"Many Gifts, One Spirit," words and music by Al Carmines, is used by permission of the author.

96 97 98 99 00 01 02 03 04 05 — 10 9 8 7 6 5 4 3 2 1

MANUFACTURED IN THE UNITED STATES OF AMERICA

For my gifted son, Stephen Henry Bauman,
the genuine thing, who calls
me to play in life and
lets me be a good
enough mom

Contents

Contents

Introduction

What are your special gifts and abilities?
What is God's plan for your life?
How is God calling you to use your specific gifts?

You are about to embark on a Spirit-led journey of discovery and growth that will help you find answers to these and other questions related to your important role in God's divine plan. In addition to helping you gain a biblical foundation for understanding spiritual gifts and their importance to the church, SpiritGifts will guide you through the process of naming, claiming, and coming to understand and appreciate your own spiritual gifts. As you work with others in your group to discover one another's gifts and challenge one another to use those gifts to meet real needs in your congregation, community, and world, you will grow spiritually and experience an increased sense of meaning and purpose in your life. And as you begin to recognize where to focus your energies and become actively involved in serving according to your specific gifts, you will be continually enabled and empowered to do God's will in your life.

SpiritGifts affirms that each individual is a holy child of God who is gifted by the Spirit. Unlike talents or abilities that can be earned or received through training, spiritual gifts are given to us by God. *Charismata* is a Greek word that means "gifts of grace." In this program we use the word *charismata* to refer to *all* of the gifts or special abilities given by God. The gifts are given for a purpose; they are intended to be used. The presence of the Holy Spirit energizes our gifts for service. In effect, *charismata* is the call of Jesus Christ to serve within the community, thus benefiting and strengthening the church with the use of specific gifts. *Charismata* is the key that unlocks the power of God to be in ministry to the world. As you and the other individuals in your group discover

Introduction

and use this key, you will see the work and ministry of the entire congregation grow.

Your SpiritGifts leader will encourage you to make a commitment to pray for one another throughout the program. Your prayer should center on a constant awareness of the holy within yourself and each person you encounter. Pray that during your time together the Spirit will be at work, helping you to discern God's will in your lives and your ministry.

SpiritGifts sets you on a course to open yourself to God in ways that will enable you to see and accept your gifts, which are spiritual realities. The process you begin is open-ended. This is only the beginning of a an exciting, lifelong journey. May you join the creative forces of the Spirit to joyfully accomplish God's gracious work and will for your life.

SpiritGifts

Many Gifts, One Spirit

1. God of change and glo - ry, God of time and space,
when we fear the fu - ture, give to us your grace.
In the midst of chang-ing ways give us still the grace to praise.

2. God of man - y col - ors, God of man - y signs,
you have made us dif - ferent, bless - ing man - y kinds.
As the old ways dis - ap - pear, let your love cast out our fear.

3. Fresh-ness of the morn - ing, new - ness of each night,
you are still cre - at - ing end - less love and light.
This we see, as shad-ows part, man - y gifts from one great heart.

WORDS: Al Carmines, 1973
MUSIC: Al Carmines, 1973
© 1974 Al Carmines

KATHERINE
65.65.77

Refrain

Man - y gifts, one Spir - it, one love known in man - y ways.

In our dif - fer - ence is bless - ing, from di - ver - si - ty we praise one Giv - er,

one Lord, one Spir - it, one Word known in man - y ways,

hal - low - ing our days. For the Giv - er, for the gifts, praise, praise, praise!

Are These the Questions You Are Asking?

* ★ What is God's will for my life?
* ★ How can I know God's purpose for my life?
* ★ How can I find fulfillment in God's world?

These important questions are for us to answer. When we name and claim our gifts, we can make intentional choices that will align us with what God would have us do and be. As we discover our spiritual gifts, God's will in our lives is also made clear.

It is by God's grace and love—not by anything we do—that we have been given gifts.

Underline five gifts named in the passage below.

Each of us was given grace according to the measure of Christ's gift. Therefore it is said,
   "When he ascended on high he made captivity itself a captive;
   he gave gifts to his people."
. . . The gifts he gave were that some would be apostles, some prophets, some evangelists, some pastors and teachers, to equip the saints for the work of ministry, for building up the body of Christ, until all of us come to the unity of the faith and of the knowledge of the Son of God, to maturity, to the measure of the full stature of Christ.

EPHESIANS 4:7-8, 11-13

We've been given our gifts to _____

_____

_____.

Other Questions to Consider

- ★ What are the gifts of the Holy Spirit?
- ★ Are these gifts real?
- ★ Are they biblically based?
- ★ Do they make sense in light of what I already understand about God?
- ★ Why do I need to know and study these gifts?
- ★ How do I know if I have a gift of the Spirit?
- ★ Once I discover my gifts, how do I use them?
- ★ Are gifts different from talents?
- ★ Are the gifts of the Spirit and the fruit of the Spirit the same?

These are questions we will be exploring together.
Do you have other questions?
Write them here.

The Work of the Spirit Within You

> Then afterward
>   I will pour out my spirit on all flesh;
> your sons and your daughters shall prophesy,
>   your old men shall dream dreams,
>   and your young men shall see visions.
> Even on the male and female slaves,
>   in those days, I will pour out my spirit.
>
> JOEL 2:28-29

_____ has been a promise of God to you since the time of the writings of the prophet Joel in the Hebrew Scriptures.

> "I baptize you with water for repentance, but one who is more powerful than I is coming after me; I am not worthy to carry his sandals. He will baptize you with the Holy Spirit and fire."
>
> MATTHEW 3:11

Just as _____ acted through the guidance and empowerment of the Holy Spirit, so can you.

> "But you will receive power when the Holy Spirit has come upon you; and you will be my witnesses in Jerusalem, in all Judea and Samaria, and to the ends of the earth."
>
> ACTS 1:8

And just as the Holy Spirit led _____

_____ through the event of Pentecost and into the first struggling days of the church's history, so you will be led and strengthened.

*   *   *   *

The Holy Spirit works to bring about _____

_____ .

The Holy Spirit _____ and

_____ us for the work of ministry within the Christian community.

The Bible and Spiritual Gifts

In SpiritGifts the gift is called . . .	Romans 12:3-8	1 Corinthians 12:4-11	1 Corinthians 12:27-31	Ephesians 4:7-16
Prophecy	prophecy	prophecy	prophets	prophets
Pastoring	ministry			pastors
Teaching	teacher		teachers	teachers
Encouragement	exhorter			
Giving	giver			
Compassion	compassionate			
Wisdom		wisdom		
Knowledge		knowledge		
Faith		faith		
Healing		healing	healing	
Miracles		miracles	power/ miracles	
Discernment		discernment		
Tongues		tongues	tongues	
Interpretation		interpretation	interpret	
Apostleship			apostles	apostles
Assisting			assistance	
Leadership	leader		leadership	
Evangelism				evangelists

Find these four scripture passages in your Bible translation. Underline the gifts with a pencil or pen as you identify them.

Responsive Listening Bible Study
(Eight Steps)

STEP 1. Read the passage slowly, with one person reading out loud. [3-4 minutes]

STEP 2. In silence, recall the word or phrase that most caught your attention and reflect on this word. [1 minute]

STEP 3. Each person shares the word or phrase with the group without comment. [1-2 minutes]

STEP 4. A different person reads the passage out loud again. [3-4 minutes]

STEP 5. Think out: "Where does this passage touch my life or our community or our nation or our world today?" Each person responds using an "I" statement (not "The church thinks . . . " or "The world thinks . . . " but "I think . . . "). [3-5 minutes]

STEP 6. A different person reads the passage out loud again. [3-4 minutes]

STEP 7. Think out: "From what I have heard and shared, what does God want me to do or be this week? How does God invite me to change?" Each person responds using an "I" statement. Share as time allows, making sure to leave time for prayer (step 8). You may want to jot down a few notes as the person on your right is speaking, so that you will remember what to pray about in step 8. [3-5 minutes]

STEP 8. One at a time, each person briefly prays out loud for the person on his or her right, naming what that person shared in step 7. The group may wish to join hands. [3-5 minutes]

NOTE: Be brief in steps 5 and 7. Do not elaborate, teach, or explain. Listen without responding. No one is to comment, critique, or build on what is said as if in a discussion group. If there is more than one group, remain in quiet reflection and prayer until everyone is finished.

Responsive Listening Bible Study

EPHESIANS 4:1-16

In the fourth chapter of Ephesians, emphasis is placed on the things that contribute to the peace, unity, and growth of the church, in contrast to actions that support the powers of division and destruction. God's mysterious intention is to unite all things in heaven and earth. By the gifts of Christ, the church is equipped for ministry and service.

I therefore, the prisoner in the Lord, beg you to lead a life worthy of the calling to which you have been called, with all humility and gentleness, with patience, bearing with one another in love, making every effort to maintain the unity of the Spirit in the bond of peace. There is one body and one Spirit, just as you were called to the one hope of your calling, one Lord, one faith, one baptism, one God and Father of all, who is above all and through all and in all.

But each of us was given grace according to the measure of Christ's gift. Therefore it is said,

"When he ascended on high he made captivity itself a captive;
he gave gifts to his people."

(When it says, "He ascended," what does it mean but that he had also descended into the lower parts of the earth? He who descended is the same one who ascended far above all the heavens, so that he might fill all things.) The gifts he gave were that some would be apostles, some prophets, some evangelists, some pastors and teachers, to equip the saints for the work of ministry, for building up the body of Christ, until all of us come to the unity of the faith and of the knowledge of the Son of God, to maturity, to the measure of the full stature of Christ. We must no longer be children, tossed to and fro and blown about by every wind of doctrine, by people's trickery, by their craftiness in deceitful scheming. But speaking the truth in love, we must grow up in every way into him who is the head, into Christ, from whom the whole body, joined and knit together by every ligament with which it is equipped, as each part is working properly, promotes the body's growth in building itself up in love.

EPHESIANS 4:1-16

SpiritGifts: Participant's Workbook

In your small groups, follow the step-by-step instructions on pages 19-20 to study Ephesians 4:1-16.

When your group has completed the Bible study, locate and underline the five gifts of the Spirit listed in the text. When you are finished, reflect on the passage in silence and wait for further instructions.

NOTES:

Why Do I Need to Know and Study the Gifts of the Holy Spirit?

It is true that many people have been living a Christian life for years without knowing about the gifts of the Holy Spirit. God's work in our lives is not entirely contingent on our knowledge or even our agreement to work with God. God has always been at work in each one of us.

But when we study, name, and claim our gifts, we can

★ _____

★ _____

Remember: God is already at work in each individual we meet.

What Is A Gift of the Holy Spirit?

A gift of the Holy Spirit is

★ a _____; it is not something

  we can _____ on our own

★ _____ and _____

  by God

★ used for the _____

★ energized by the _____

★ used in obedience to _____

★ for the healing of _____

  _____

How Can I Search Out My Gifts?

How do we go about discerning and naming the gifts that the Holy Spirit has set upon us? Here are three steps to guide you.

1. _____

2. _____

3. _____

God Is Always with Me

List one to five events in your life in which you have felt God's presence. These are times when you have felt God very near and close to you. They may have been spiritual mountaintop highs or simply ordinary times in your life.

1. _____

2. _____

3. _____

4. _____

5. _____

How have you seen God's faithfulness as you look back at your life? Do you sense any pattern or common thread in God's revealing presence? As you discern your gifts during SpiritGifts, how might you know that God is revealing them to you? What clues, if any, have you uncovered?

Find a partner and discuss.

NOTES:

Gifts and God's Will

1. Each one of us has been given _____.

Each one of us has been given gifts by the Holy Spirit. We can use these gifts to live in peace with God's purpose for our lives. We can employ these gifts to take our place and be an active part in God's wonderful plan for the world. Our choice is simple. We have the wonderful invitation to be a part of God's work in reconciling and reuniting the world. When we work toward that cause, we are God's people.

2. You have _____ as a unique child of God.

God wants you to use your gifts to live God's plan for your life. Your gifts are unique. Because you have particular gifts as a unique child of God, your gifts influence the specific ways in which you respond to God's call in your life. Your gifts shape the way you live your life.

3. Using your spiritual gifts brings you _____!

How can the gifts of the Holy Spirit within you bring you deep joy? As you use and live within the gifts of God, you have a sense of doing what you were created to do and of being who you were created to be. You affirm your best self, as God planned for you to be. You find satisfaction and happiness as you do particular things well. You act on your values and beliefs. You see your deepest longings and hopes fulfilled as you use your gifts effectively to achieve realistic goals. God may ask you to stretch your potential, but God will not ask you to do things that are not true to who you are. Remember that each one of the gifts can be lived out in a number of ways.

4. Reaching your _____

is God's plan.

As you use your gifts, you begin to understand that reaching your potential is more important than reaching the goal or goals you have set. If you are successful by the world's standards but are unfaithful to what is true and right and of God, then you fail in your efforts as a disciple.

As you discern and use your gifts, you enter an exciting experience of self-discovery. You find new opportunities to use the full potential of your life. It is exciting to know that you can be a part of God's plan to renew the world!

When I Live in God's Will

1. When I live in God's will, _____

_____.

Knowing our gifts helps us to know where to place our time and energy. We begin to prioritize our tasks and jobs, no longer overcome by the thought that everything is of equal importance to serve God and the community.

2. When I live in God's will, _____

_____.

Identifying our gifts and telling others what our gifts are help us to say "no." In this way we can have the time and resources free to say "yes" when we can contribute our very best.

3. When I live in God's will, _____

_____.

When we name and claim our gifts and then agree to do the tasks and jobs that fall under those gifts, we feel revitalized and energized to do the work and more. Of course, if we overwork our gifts and don't take care of ourselves, burnout can still result.

4. When I live in God's will, _____

_____.

When we accomplish a task or project that we know God has called and equipped us to do, we feel good about the work and ourselves. Our self-esteem is lifted, and we find pleasure in the dignity of our work, the elegance of its simplicity, and the essential responsibility in serving others.

Spiritual Gifts Survey

Rank each of the following statements as it applies to your experience or inclination.

Much (3), Some (2), Little (1), or None (0).

This is a self survey, not a test. There are no right or wrong answers. Therefore, be sure to let your responses reflect your opinions of yourself. This survey will not be shared except as you choose.

_____ 1. I make a point to be with people of other cultures and ethnic backgrounds.

_____ 2. I see destructive patterns in people's lives and help them to find healthier ways of living.

_____ 3. I listen as other people tell me about their religious experiences and spiritual journeys.

_____ 4. People often seek me out and ask me to pray with them.

_____ 5. I can explain in simple ways complex ideas about God and how to live as a disciple.

_____ 6. I often praise coworkers for their good work and attitudes.

_____ 7. I carefully get all the information I need before moving into action.

_____ 8. I can share deep truths with others about their problems.

_____ 9. When I see a need, I spring to action and do something about it.

Much (3), Some (2), Little (1), or None (0).

_____ 10. I am materially blessed, and I give what I can to others freely.

_____ 11. Being in charge doesn't mean I have to control everything.

_____ 12. I can sit and simply listen to someone who needs a listening ear.

_____ 13. I do the best I can and leave the rest in God's hands.

_____ 14. I speak up and tell others when I don't believe they are telling the whole truth.

_____ 15. I have experienced times when something miraculously happened that was contrary to natural law.

_____ 16. I look for opportunities to bring hope and God's comfort to those who are sick.

_____ 17. I have spoken in verbal utterances that praise God but are not understandable by human ears.

_____ 18. I have been able to learn foreign languages easily.

_____ 19. My circle of friends looks like a meeting of the United Nations.

_____ 20. I am energized when I speak about what needs to be changed in church and other arenas.

_____ 21. Inviting others to join me in something I enjoy is something I do every week.

_____ 22. I find myself time and again listening to people's spiritual struggles and offering guidance.

Much (3), Some (2), Little (1), or None (0).

_____ 23. When I am a student in a class or the teacher of a class, other participants are energized and motivated.

_____ 24. I am able to work with people and help them do their best.

_____ 25. I am able to grasp deep truths about God and make sense of them.

_____ 26. I am able to use my knowledge in complex situations, weighing the pros and cons, and know what is right.

_____ 27. I don't mind lending a hand and doing the trivial jobs that are often overlooked.

_____ 28. I give 10 percent of my income and more to my church and other charitable needs.

_____ 29. When I am working on a group project, I make the extra effort to communicate with everyone.

_____ 30. Stopping what I am doing to help someone in need is a normal part of my day.

_____ 31. When I believe that something is of God, I act boldly on my belief.

_____ 32. My friends often ask me to help sort out what is real and what is phony.

_____ 33. God has mysteriously intervened in extraordinary ways in my presence.

_____ 34. I am able to counsel others to help restore them to mental and spiritual health.

Much (3), Some (2), Little (1), or None (0).

____ 35. I have spoken in a language that I am not normally able to speak.

____ 36. I can hear verbal sounds not understood by others and understand what is meant.

____ 37. I rejoice that our church has such a wide diversity of people.

____ 38. I can see change coming and am not afraid to help people make the needed changes.

____ 39. Sharing how I became a Christian comes naturally for me.

____ 40. I can be called upon when someone needs help in making difficult decisions.

____ 41. I am good at giving directions to people so that they can complete projects successfully.

____ 42. I make a point to say a kind word to those whose abilities I admire.

____ 43. I am deeply satisfied when I study in order to explain hard concepts to others.

____ 44. I don't panic in difficult situations, but weigh all the circumstances to find a solution.

____ 45. I'd rather stay in the background doing the labor than be out front speaking or teaching.

____ 46. I spend a lot of time earning and raising money and an equal amount of time giving it away.

Much (3), Some (2), Little (1), or None (0).

____ 47. I am good at organizing and leading a group to meet their goals.

____ 48. I walk gently with people who are grieving, and can walk with them in their process of healing.

____ 49. I live the best I can each day, one day at a time, not worrying about tomorrow.

____ 50. I can "see through" people and circumstances and know what is real and what is not.

____ 51. Time and again I have seen miracles, acts contrary to natural law, occur.

____ 52. I am able to help, comfort, and counsel when people are deeply troubled.

____ 53. I have had the experience of "speaking in tongues."

____ 54. I am able to move into another culture, speak another language, and feel at home.

Spiritual Gifts Survey Answer Sheet

Transfer your responses from the survey to this answer sheet. Add the total at the end of each line. Remember, this survey reflects only your past history and not what God may be doing even now in this moment or will do in your future.

Gift		*Responses*		*Total*
APOSTLESHIP	1	19	37	
PROPHECY	2	20	38	
EVANGELISM	3	21	39	
PASTORING	4	22	40	
TEACHING	5	23	41	
ENCOURAGEMENT	6	24	42	
KNOWLEDGE	7	25	43	
WISDOM	8	26	44	
ASSISTING	9	27	45	
GIVING	10	28	46	
LEADERSHIP	11	29	47	
COMPASSION	12	30	48	
FAITH	13	31	49	
DISCERNMENT	14	32	50	
MIRACLES	15	33	51	
HEALING	16	34	52	
TONGUES	17	35	53	
INTERPRETATION	18	36	54	

My Top Three Gifts

List your top three gifts in the order of highest numerical value as indicated by the survey sheet. **Please list only three.**

First

_____

Second

_____

Third

_____

List one more gift that you sense may be yours

_____

Now proceed to page 37. Begin reading about the gifts that may be yours.

Gifts of the Spirit: Descriptions

The gifts are divided into three categories: gifts of word, gifts of deed, and gifts of sign. This reminds us that we are disciples who live the ways of Christ in

> what we say (**word**),
> what we do (**deed**),
> ways and signs that point to God (**sign**).

Division between the categories of word, deed, and sign are not always clear-cut. A person may live out a gift in one, two, or all three of these ways. For instance, a woman with the gift of evangelism tells a friend about Jesus (word) as she works at the homeless shelter sorting clothing (deed). A man with the gift of healing works as a physician's assistant in a hospital (deed) even as he prays with and comforts a preoperative patient (sign). A gift may demonstrate the ways of Christ in more than one way.

As you study the gifts, you probably will find that you have more than one. A number of gifts may be yours. Often gifts interconnect and complement each other.

Gifts of Word

Apostleship

The gift of apostleship does not mean that you are to become like one of the original twelve apostles. Instead let's look specifically to the example of Paul, who was also named an apostle. He was a missionary to the church. As a missionary apostle he was **called out by God and sent to a specific people.** He was able to **cross cultural boundaries** to reach people for Jesus Christ and **form new Christian communities.**

Prophecy

This gift does not imply that you should get a nine-hundred number and set up your own psychic hot line or go buy a pack of tarot cards! The word *prophet* means "forth-teller." Think of a prophet as one who can **know past history, see present occurrences, and then understand the bigger picture. A prophet is called to instruct, warn, correct, and forecast the end result.**

Evangelism

Get off your soapbox and put away your bullhorn! Think of people, both introverts and extroverts, shy and outgoing, who **can communicate the gospel message through word and deed.** Are you able to share the good news of Jesus Christ in ways so that people can see, hear, and accept it? Then you may have the gift of evangelism.

Pastoring

This gift is also referred to as shepherding, but don't go buy a herd of sheep. Instead, pull out your **abilities to be a spiritual guide, to sustain people on their journeys, and to work with those who are at different places on the discipleship road.**

Teaching

You don't need a college degree to have the gift of teaching. And just because you are capable of teaching doesn't mean you automatically have the gift. Spiritual teachers have the **ability to clearly explain and effectively apply the truth of Jesus Christ.** Remember, people watch teachers more than others to see if their lifestyles are consistent with their lessons.

Encouragement

The word used in the Bible is *exhortation,* but a more understandable term for us is the word *encouragement.* **Do you come alongside persons to help? Do you work with the lesser able and** undergird people to use and do their very best? This is not a "fix it" person but one who "travels with" another.

Knowledge

Having the gift of knowledge is not being the champion on the popular TV show *Jeopardy* or a winner at Trivial Pursuit. Instead it is **a supernatural ability to stretch beyond the facts and figures to search, make sense of, and bring together the teachings of God for people's lives.**

Wisdom

Wisdom means putting what you know to work in your daily life and helping others to do the same. It is **being in tune with the heart of God** and then living that way. A person with the gift of wisdom weighs all the circumstances in complex situations to find the deeper truth.

Gifts of Deed

Assisting

This gift should carry a warning: "This is not the business of the things we think we *should* do." But if you are one who **assists and lends a helping hand in times of need,** this may be your gift. Do you feel called to give leadership in the distribution of supplies in a disaster area, do the leg work for a group project, or make needed deliveries? Then you may have this gift of assisting and helping others.

Giving

Don't think that if you don't have this gift it means you can ignore the offering plate the next time it's passed! We all are commanded to give. We all have received so much from God that we can't help wanting to give in return. But those with the giving gift **give freely, with a special measure and delight to further God's work in the world.** You also don't have to be rich to have the gift. Remember the Bible story about the widow's mite (Mark 12:41-44)?

Leadership

If you are controlling, domineering, and *need* to be a leader, this gift is not for you! Some Bible translations use the word *government* to name this gift. These gifted individuals are able to **share information and power.** They **enable those around them to realize and accomplish their goals.** They are good managers and administrators. These persons take leadership roles to equip the church, the Christian community, to work in ways that bring about *God's will.*

Compassion

There are many of us who easily show emotion, but the **ability to empathize with others, stand in their shoes, and then act in ways that help them on their journey** is the essence of the gift of mercy and compassion.

Faith

The Spirit-given **ability to daily see God's will, coupled with the confidence to do it,** is the gift of faith. It is living one day at a time even when life seems out of control. To live fully in faith is to live each day as best you can for who you are in that moment and to trust the rest to God.

Gifts of Sign

Discernment

This is a special ability to **distinguish between truth and error, justice and injustice, what is authentic and genuine and what is phony.** You are able to "see through" people or circumstances to know what is real and what is an illusion, and you have the wisdom and courage to speak or reveal the truth.

Miracles

Are you ready for a miracle? Those with this Spirit-given power are able to **act contrary to natural law or use natural law in**

extraordinary ways. This gift is displayed when God's hand miraculously intervenes in your presence in extraordinary ways.

Healing

This is the ability to allow God to work through you as **an instrument for the curing of illness and the restoration of persons' physical, mental, and spiritual health.** (Note of caution: The cure does not depend on the receiving person's faith or the healer's amount of faith.)

Tongues

The sign should read, "NOT FOR CHARISMATICS ONLY." The book of Acts in the New Testament records that on the Day of Pentecost, the tongues spoken were **different languages that normally would not have been spoken** by the people (Acts 2:6). Other times tongues are understood as **verbal utterances that praise God but are not understood by human ears.** Whichever it is, it is a gift to be prized.

Interpretation

Linguistics might be your bag! The gift of interpretation is **the ability to translate when a foreign language is uttered. In a time when we must cross all cultural and language boundaries, this is an invaluable gift.** In the case of ecstatic utterances, as when someone is speaking in tongues, the gift of interpretation can mean to **interpret the nonlinguistic sounds so that the message is understood.**

> NOTE: The gift of tongues and the gift of interpretation have sometimes been misunderstood. They are legitimate gifts even though in some places and at some times they may not be as commonly evident as some of the other gifts. Keep an open mind as you continue to study these gifts so that you can remain open to the Spirit's work in your own and others' lives.

Some Bible Basics

1. God Gives Gifts to Everyone.

> Now there are varieties of gifts, but the same Spirit; and there are
> varieties of services, but the same Lord; and there are varieties of
> activities, but it is the same God who activates all of them in every-
> one. To each is given the manifestation of the Spirit for the com-
> mon good.
>
> 1 CORINTHIANS 12:4-7

Notes: _____

_____

_____

2. God Distributes the Gifts According to God's Grace.

> The gifts he gave were that some would be apostles, some
> prophets, some evangelists, some pastors and teachers, to equip the
> saints for the work of ministry, for building up the body of Christ.
>
> EPHESIANS 4:11-12

Notes: _____

_____

_____

3. God Promises the Holy Spirit Will Be Our Comforter and Guide.

> "I have said these things to you while I am still with you. But the Advocate, the Holy Spirit, whom the Father will send in my name, will teach you everything, and remind you of all that I have said to you. Peace I leave with you."
>
> JOHN 14:25-27a

Notes: _____

_____

_____

Biblical and Contemporary Examples of the Gifts

Apostleship

In the Bible

When we think of apostles, we usually think of the twelve followers called by Jesus during his earthly ministry (see Matthew 10:2). As we read in the Bible, however, the title apostle also was extended to other key leaders in the Christian movement, such as Barnabas and Paul (see Acts 14:14). In Ephesians 3:1-13, Paul claims to be the least of the apostles, commissioned by God's grace. Acts 1:21-26 tells us of another apostle, Matthias, who was chosen to take the place of Judas in ministry. And in Acts 5:12-16, unnamed apostles performed signs and wonders of healing among the people.

In the Bible, persons with the gift of apostleship are missionaries. The Greek word *apostolos* and the Latin word *mission* mean "one who is sent" or "messenger." A missionary is one who lives as Jesus did, as a missional itinerant. Persons with the gift of apostleship are able to minister in a second culture. They give effective leadership in new places for the purpose of teaching the gospel, starting new congregations, and training and enabling leaders. They work to extend God's realm of justice. Second Corinthians 12:12 reminds us that they are persons of outstanding patience. However, as we read in 1 Corinthians 4:8-13, the gift of apostleship is not without cost: apostles are spectacles to the world, fools for the sake of Christ, and are hungry, poorly clothed, and held in disrepute.

Today

Today a person with the gift of apostleship might be called a pioneer missionary. Roben is such a missionary who serves in the inner city. Living in a parsonage next door to her congregation, she sees the hard street life of drugs and violence. Yet Roben, who is a single parent of two young children, feels called to minister there. Roben, an Anglo, reaches out in the name of Christ to her Spanish-speaking neighborhood. By playing midnight basketball with African American and Hispanic males, she establishes God's presence. She shares Christ's love through contemporary worship with the gay and lesbian community. She is in ministry with the people. Roben is truly a person with the gift of apostleship.

Prophecy

In the Bible

Persons who receive and communicate a message from God have the gift of prophecy. They have a special ability to listen to God. Prophets see and speak the will of God for a specific people, time, and place. In the book of Acts we find several examples of the gift of prophecy. In Acts 11:27-28, Agabus, a follower of Christ, predicts there will be a severe famine throughout the region—a prediction that later comes true. In Acts 20:10, Paul bends over a gravely ill man and rightly announces that the man will live. Acts 21:9 tells us that Philip, the evangelist, had four daughters, all with the gift of prophecy.

The book of Acts also portrays the disciple Peter's use of the gift of prophecy. In chapters 1 and 2, Peter repeatedly uses the Hebrew Scripture to validate his spoken truths. Later, in chapter 5, he is able to identify evil motives of Ananias and Sapphira, who lied to the congregation about what they had given. We see that Peter is bold and forthright with others concerning God's demands on their lives, directing them to align their lives with God and leading them to repentance and baptism.

Like Peter, persons with the gift of prophecy possess a burning desire to serve by proclaiming God's truth. Prophets have a strong sense of duty, yet they must remember to temper their gift of prophecy with love so that they do more good than harm.

Today

When we think of the prophetic voices of this century, Dr. Martin Luther King Jr. comes to mind. Dr. King was a man of God who had a dream. He spoke out on freedom, nonviolence, and civil rights in a thoughtful, intelligent, and provocative manner. He was determined to achieve justice and equality for all people. His message is as relevant today as it was during his lifetime. Persons throughout the world continue to be inspired by his vision, passion, and faith. Through his commitment, courage, and dedication, he is esteemed as a prophet for our time.

Evangelism

In the Bible

The gift of evangelism enables persons to reach beyond their usual sphere of influence to share the gospel and God's love. Peter, by word and example, does so in Acts 2:14-21. Evangelists are able to help others see their lives clearly in the context of God's grace, moving them to life-changing decisions. They realize they cannot take credit for a person coming to faith because it is God's doing, as we read in 1 Corinthians 3:5-9. Through the ministry of evangelists, seekers come to know the truth (see 1 Timothy 2:1-7), place their faith in God, and become Jesus' disciples. Yet the gift of evangelism does not end there. People with this gift go on to help persons become grounded and formed as Christian disciples.

In Acts 8:4-8, the disciple Philip demonstrates the gift of evangelism while in Samaria. The people accept Christ as they are "hearing and seeing the signs that he did." Philip witnesses as he proclaims the good news and cures the lame. In another story, found in Acts 8:26-40, Philip evangelizes a man from Ethiopia who works for the queen. Together they study the Scriptures. The Ethiopian asks Philip, "What is to prevent me from being baptized?" Philip baptizes the man who has accepted Christ as the new ruler of his life.

Today

Leon is a man with a mission, a mission that began with a yearning to reach out to men in prison. Today he has engineered the first Kairos prison ministry* in his state. Through a three-day in-house spiritual retreat, these incarcerated men hear, many for the first time, about the love of Christ and their own worthiness. They come to understand that Christ came to earth so that they might live. Leon also is the leader of an out-prison ministry that assists released prisoners to get on their feet. He not only has the ability to organize, but he also is able to share a vision that catches other people's attention and energy. Leon demonstrates his passionate love of people as he shares the greatest gift of all: Jesus.

Pastoring

In the Bible

As we read in 1 Timothy 3:1-7, those with the gift of pastoring are able to counsel and encourage followers. They are able to mentor others in their discipleship journeys because they have already traveled the road. They take responsibility to care for a group of believers over the long haul. Like the follower Titus, they use Scripture reading and teaching to reinforce their preaching (see Titus 1:9). They call persons to accountable discipleship and intercede when someone wanders away from holy living. They keep a watchful eye for the well-being of others. These spiritual, people-centered persons patiently pray for others, desiring them to grow spiritually as disciples.

In Jesus we see the heart of a pastor. John 14 illustrates Jesus' pastoring characteristics. In verse 9, Jesus shows the disciples the error of their way. In verses 11-14, he patiently shares truth with them as he senses they are able to hear and accept it. Then he

---

*An adaptation of the Roman Catholic Cursillo, Episcopalian Cursillo, Tres Dias, and the Walk of Emmaus, Kairos prison ministry is an ecumenical project in which volunteers minister with incarcerated persons.

teaches them of the Holy Spirit in verses 16 and 17. Throughout the Gospels we see that Jesus cares for the spiritual well-being of his primary disciples, as well as for many other friends in ministry, including Mary and Martha. Jesus is the Great Shepherd.

Today

Diedra has been a seminary professor for many years. Her office and home are welcome places for students and faculty. She demonstrates tough love as she shares unqualified acceptance with those who come to her door. As a teacher of the Word, she draws on the Holy Scriptures to call persons to accountability. Diedra is a woman in touch with her own spirituality. She asks frequently, through her words and actions, if all is "well with your soul." She cares deeply for all those entrusted to her care.

Teaching

In the Bible

Persons with the gift of teaching have the ability to bring new believers into maturity. They live God's will through personal study and teaching others. They communicate in a manner that brings persons to understand and apply the learnings. This leads to informed, healthy ministry within the congregation. They teach disciples how to live in just ways. Persons with the gift of teaching also teach other teachers, so that even more persons may learn. In this way the Word is passed from person to person and generation to generation.

Acts 2:42 shows that teaching was a foundational act of the early church. Barnabas was a teacher in both Antioch and Tarsus. As we read in Acts 11:24, "he was a good man, full of the Holy Spirit and of faith." Through his gift he brought Christ to a great many people. He and Paul spent an entire year with one congregation in Antioch. It was there that the disciples were first called Christians.

Today

Patricia leads spiritual formation workshops and seminars. She is frequently asked, "What are your gifts?" The one gift she names without hesitation is teaching. She finds as much joy in preparation as she does in presentation.

Acknowledging her gift as a wonderful opportunity and a tremendous responsibility, she works hard to prepare her lessons. She uses the best methodologies so that those in her care will be able to gain spiritual content and wisdom. Patricia always recalls James's warning: "Not many of you should become teachers, my brothers and sisters, for you know that we who teach will be judged with greater strictness" (James 3:1). Therefore she always seeks divine guidance. The true test of a teacher is her or his life.

Encouragement

In the Bible

Comfort, consolation, and counsel are three primary roles of the gift of encouragement. Persons with this gift care for others in ways that empower them to be helped and healed. Encouragement is modeled in 1 Thessalonians 2:11 as a parental role. The apostle Paul writes, "We dealt with each one of you like a father with his children, urging and encouraging you and pleading that you lead a life worthy of God." As we read in Acts 14:22, encouragement was esteemed as most important to the community in times of persecution.

Timothy, an early church leader, had the gift of encouragement. We read in 2 Timothy 1:5 how his grandmother, Eunice, and mother, Lois—both women with the gift of encouragement—had first nurtured him as a child. In his First Letter to Timothy, the apostle Paul refers to Timothy's gift of encouragement as well as demonstrates his own use of the gift of encouragement: "Until I arrive, give attention to the public reading of scripture, to exhorting, to teaching. Do not neglect the gift that is in you" (4:13-14*a*). Paul's enduring relationship with Timothy encouraged and strengthened him during difficult times. Because of his gift of encouragement, Timothy was Paul's closest companion.

Today

Jeanette, a woman in full-time ministry, is filled with the gift of encouragement. She oversees the daily work of pastors entrusted to her care. She travels from congregation to congregation and house to house giving words of inspiration and comfort. She motivates those who need a bit of a push and comforts others who need reassurance. She exemplifies the charge in 1 Thessalonians 5:14 to "admonish the idlers, encourage the faint hearted, help the weak, be patient with all of them." Through a visit, letter, or phone call, she follows the Romans 12:15 instruction to "rejoice with those who rejoice, weep with those who weep."

Knowledge

In the Bible

As we read in Colossians 2:2, persons with the gift of knowledge are able to perceive and understand the mystery of God's will and ways. They have an earnest hunger to know divine, timeless truths. These truths are linked to the call for justice and righteousness. Knowledge is important for the health and well-being of the Body of Christ. In 1 Corinthians 12 we see that wisdom and knowledge are closely related. Paul prays in Colossians 1:9 that "you may be filled with the knowledge of God's will in all spiritual wisdom and understanding." Through his own gift of knowledge, Paul is able to acquire deep insight into divine truth.

Today

David is a person who searches, systematizes, and summarizes the teachings of God. His ability is closely related to the gift of teaching. In fact, he is an excellent teacher. David does not have knowledge at the expense of common sense. Instead, his knowledge directs his experience. David equips others for the work of ministry by sharing his gift of knowledge so that they can "grow in the grace and knowledge of our Lord and Savior Jesus Christ" (2 Peter 3:18). Through his efforts, numerous young people have entered full-time ministry.

Wisdom

In the Bible

When God reveals insight or direction about a particular problem to a person, that person has the gift of wisdom. Persons with this gift link their understandings of life with keen insights into the ways of God. In this way they know what to do and how to do it. First Corinthians 1:25 and 3:18-19 remind those with the gift of wisdom that God's wisdom is stronger than human wisdom. In Acts 6:3-4, seven men are selected, "full of the Spirit and of wisdom," to care for the needs of the whole community. Persons with the gift of wisdom are able to use information at the right time, in the right way. They reason and solve problems according to God's will.

Today

Dale is a man of wisdom. He uses his gift of insight and accumulated knowledge as he advocates world peace. Dale understands how knowledge and experience can be applied to specific needs of the world. He is able to grasp and order the deep truths of God's world. As he meets with governmental policy makers, he relates these truths to the needs and problems of life. Speaking on behalf of world peace before large audiences, he has the ability to apply his wisdom to complex situations. He weighs the true nature of the situation and then exercises spiritual insight into its rightness or wrongness. Dale uses his gift of wisdom as a maker of peace.

Assisting

In the Bible

Persons with the gift of assisting have the ability to bring support to those in need. In 1 Timothy 3:8, assisters called "deacons" are called to be "serious, not double-tongued, not indulging in much wine, not greedy for money; they must hold fast to the mystery of the faith with a clear conscience." Phoebe, a deacon named in Romans 16:1-2, demonstrates this special gift by giving aid to others so that they can increase the effective use of their own gifts. In 2 Timothy 1:16, Paul grants a special blessing upon the household of Onesiphorus because of his work of enablement.

Assisters sense a need and give support for the greater good of the community. In the book of Philippians, Epaphroditus offers his gift of assisting with a spirit of eagerness and joy. The text tells us how he "came close to death for the work of Christ." As Epaphroditus recognized, sometimes the gift can even demand that one lay down her or his life for another.

Today

Sally and Simon, now in their eighties, have lived a lifetime helping others. Sally is always ready to cut out the hand work for a busy Sunday school teacher, prepare a church mailing, deliver flowers, or prepare the Lord's Supper. Simon, also a ready aid, has served as a trustee for many years. Always close at hand, he helps neighbors in need, delivers meals to the elderly, ushers at the Sunday service, paints the fellowship hall, hangs a window, or stops a leaky faucet. Simon's and Sally's work frees others to serve more effectively. Their congregation and community are blessed by their gift.

Giving

In the Bible

Persons with the gift of giving have the special ability to give cheerfully and liberally to support the ongoing work of God. They are able to harness and manage monetary resources in ways that give power to further God's business. They give with simplicity, as described in Romans 12:8. Their joy and eagerness are unsurpassed as they follow the command of Christ in Matthew 6:3: "Do not let your left hand know what your right hand is doing." Barnabas is singled out for special mention in the book of Acts. In 4:34-37 we read how he sells land and brings the money to the apostles. Persons with the gift of giving benefit others and aid the work of God's reign in the world.

Today

Glenn and Bette are esteemed models of the gift of giving. Whether it's handing out food, collecting blankets for the homeless, or buying ice cream for the neighborhood children, they give such care and cheer that the recipients are fortified. It is not that they have many possessions. Rather, they share what they do have with any who are in need. These two believers are special stewards. They have discovered this Spirit-bestowed gift and derive genuine joy from seeing God work through their gift. They delight in using temporal possessions for God's glory and their neighbors' good.

Leadership

In the Bible

Persons with this gift are able to lead others effectively. In 1 Timothy 3:5, the apostle Paul gives Timothy some common sense related to recruiting leaders: "For if someone does not know how to manage his own household, how can he take care of God's church?"

God-empowered leaders have the ability to elicit trust. Persons with the gift share the vision of God's *shalom* in ways that capture the imagination. They use their leadership energies and skills for the good of the community. They set goals and communicate the desired results to others. They do all of these things so that God's will is accomplished.

Leaders care for the spiritual well-being of persons entrusted to their care. Hebrews 13:17 says that leaders "are keeping watch over your souls and will give an account. Let them do this with joy and not with sighing." Those with the gift create "safe space" for others to function and use their unique spiritual gifts.

Today

Susan is a woman of conviction who has the gift of leadership. In her work, her congregation, or her immediate family, Susan helps groups work harmoniously to accomplish their goals. Plans run smoothly as she thoughtfully considers the pros and cons of decisions, big and little. This gifted woman is able to mobilize people to accomplish God's mission and ministry. She can claim the New Testament compliment found in 1 Timothy 5:17: "Let the elders who rule well be considered worthy of double honor, especially those who labor in preaching and teaching."

Compassion

In the Bible

Tabitha was a disciple who had the gift of compassion. We learn in Acts 9:36 that throughout her hometown of Joppa she "was devoted to good works and acts of charity." The gift of compassion enabled her to have genuine empathy for others, both Christians and non-Christians. She joyfully translated her compassion into good works. Her deeds of kindness reflect God's love.

Like Tabitha, persons with the gift of compassion have a special ability to work with the afflicted, poor, and abused. They care for the "least of these," as Jesus taught his followers in Matthew 25:42-45.

Today

Mother Teresa is known by many for her gift of compassion. For years she has worked with the poorest of India. In addition to her continuing work in Calcutta, she travels the globe as a spokesperson for the outcast and downtrodden of the world. We often see pictures of her sincerely smiling into the camera or bending lovingly over a person in need. She does not work grudgingly or out of a sense of duty alone. She is a constant source of inspiration to all and an exceptional example of a person with the gift of compassion.

Faith

In the Bible

The entire chapter of Hebrews 11 describes the gift of faith in detail: "Now faith is the assurance of things hoped for, the conviction of things not seen" (v. 1). Persons with the gift of faith have extraordinary confidence in God's faithfulness. Because of their gift, they help the faith community find assurance as they do the work of ministry. Jesus teaches about faith in Matthew 17:20: "For truly I tell you, if you have faith the size of a mustard seed, you will say to this mountain, 'Move from here to there,' and it will move; and nothing will be impossible for you." Persons with this gift may not desire to move physical mountains, but through their gift they enable the church to "keep on keeping on" in faithfulness to God's calling.

Today

Ada would be the last to boast of having the gift of faith. Instead, she sees herself as a woman who has done the best she can through the years and left the rest in God's hands. She prays that God will find her worthy when the trumpet sounds for her to return home. In her eighty-plus years, Ada has raised seven children and buried a coal mining husband who died of black lung. Through the lean times, she has cared for herself and her family. In faith to Christ, she has given generous aid to her home congregation, helped to establish the local fire department, and cared for other community needs. When her home and small country store serving a backwoods community burned down, she picked through the rubble and began again. Her community respects her, and her children and grandchildren call her blessed. Ada is a woman of faith.

Discernment

In the Bible

Persons with the gift of discernment are able to look beyond certain behaviors and circumstances to determine if they are good or evil, right or wrong. They call persons to accountability, as Jesus does in Matthew 7:5: "You hypocrite, first take the log out of your own eye, and then you will see clearly to take the speck out of your neighbor's eye." They look through apparent issues and see underlying truths. They make judgments concerning what is and what is not of God. In Acts 5:1-6, the apostle Peter brings to accountability two persons who have lied to the community.

Persons with the gift of discernment bring health and wholeness to the community of Christ. Because they are able to analyze what inclinations should be encouraged and what tendencies should be discouraged in brothers and sisters of the faith, they are valuable in personal counseling situations. In 1 John 4:1 we read, "Beloved, do not believe every spirit, but test the spirits to see whether they are from God." Some persons with the gift are able to perform this task better than others.

Today

Al is a person with the gift of discernment. Because of his keen insights, leaders appreciate having Al attend their meetings. He calls group dynamics into question and asks persons to be accountable for their actions. Al "sees through" persons to the spiritual needs within. He picks up subtle hints that tell him when people are at odds with what they are saying. Having the ability to see through the facade, he differentiates between what is raised up by God and what pretends to be. He has the uncanny ability to unmask false teachings and ways. Al is valuable in helping others pinpoint and assess their gifts to find their niche in the mission and ministry of the community. Al is an excellent spiritual mentor and guide.

Miracles

In the Bible

Three words are used in the Bible in connection with miracles: power, wonder, and sign. Acts 5:12 states: "Now many signs and wonders were done among the people through the apostles." In the most restrictive interpretation, persons with the gift of miracles participate with God to do powerful works that transcend and alter the ordinary course of nature as we know it. These supernatural works demonstrate God's love and power. In Acts 5:15-16, Peter casts a shadow that heals many. Observers perceive that the ordinary course of fate has been altered. After Tabitha, a godly woman, dies, Peter raises her from the dead. Likewise, in Acts 20:7-12, Paul revives Eutychus, a young man who has fallen to his death. True miracles, like these, are palpable to the senses. Acts 8:6-8 reports the sign miracles that the disciple Philip accorded. Miracles are evidence in order to authenticate the divine commission to bring in the reign and realm of God. In a broader sense, miracles are an unusual and timely providential interference in human affairs. Persons with this gift witness remarkable answers to prayer, extra strength in times of need, abundant provision in scarcity, and timely protection in danger. These human intermediaries are able to help free others from what prevents them from fulfilling their ministry. These blockages are related to the body, mind, and spirit.

Today

Pamela has witnessed miracles in her presence many times. She acknowledges that God does not usually choose miracles to intervene in our lives, yet, as a hospital chaplain at a major medical center, she does not deny the evidence of their occurrences. She never tries to explain away a miracle. Instead, she accepts miracles for what they are: signs of God's continuous presence and activity in the world.

Pamela reminds us that Jesus' calming the sea was important, but not any more remarkable than calming the anxious hearts of loved ones as they sit at the deathbed of their beloved mother. Feeding the four thousand was grand, but how beneficial it is for the hungry children of Rwanda finally to receive long awaited food supplies. Raising the dead is amazing, but how marvelous it is to witness a person, once dying from drugs and alcohol, receive eternal life. Jesus promised his followers would "do greater works than these" (John 14:12). This promise is being fulfilled today. Those deaf to God hear the Word. The lame begin to walk in righteousness. The selfish find new purpose, and those who do wrong make restitution.

Healing

In the Bible

Numerous examples of healing power, worked through Jesus Christ during his ministry on earth, are recorded in Scripture. A paralyzed man is lowered down to Jesus through a roof and later walks out (Luke 5:17-26), a rich man's servant is cured (Matthew 8:5-13), and one with a withered hand is revived with a touch (Mark 3:1-6)—all testifying to Jesus' abilities. Matthew 9:35 states: "Jesus went about all the cities and villages . . . curing every disease and every sickness."

The gift of healing continued in the works of the disciples after Jesus' death. Peter healed a lame man (Acts 3:6-8), Stephen did great signs and wonders of healing (Acts 6:8), Philip cured those of unclean spirits (Acts 8:5-8), Paul healed a crippled person in Lystra (Acts 14:8-10), and many healing miracles occurred in the city of Ephesus (Acts 19:11-12). Persons with the gift of healing have the ability to cure or be cured of ill conditions that hinder effective ministries for Christ, the church, or other persons.

Today

David, a layperson, felt led to begin a healing ministry and worship service in his church. David takes seriously the instructions in James 5:14-16: "Are any among you sick? They should call for the elders of the church and have them pray over them, anointing them with oil in the name of the Lord" (v. 14).

Through his ministry, David has witnessed many healings. He realizes that healings happen through those who are open to God working in their lives. He is willing to serve as a human intermediary for the healing of himself and others. Many have come to David, either through worship services or in one-on-one visits. They have been cured of illness and restored to health. They are witnesses to God's healing power which brings wholeness to one's mind, body, and spirit.

Other persons within David's congregation also have named and claimed healing as their gift. Although David was the first to acknowledge God's work through his life, evidenced by healing, now others join him in this ministry. A counseling center has been opened in the church. A spiritual network is in place, helping persons learn disciplined spiritual formation. An Alcoholics Anonymous group recently started meeting in the church's education building. Spiritual and physical health are being restored, not only in the immediate congregation but also within the broader community.

Tongues

In the Bible

The biblical gift of tongues is manifested in two ways. In Acts 2:1-13 it seems to refer to a foreign language. On the day of Pentecost, the disciples spoke in dialects that were not their native tongues. They received a message from God and, through a divinely anointed utterance, communicated it with others in languages the disciples themselves had never learned. This occurred so that people from many nations could hear the message of Christ.

A second use of the gift of tongues appears in 1 Corinthians 12–14. Here we see persons with the ability to speak in an unknown language for private devotion and edification. Speaking in tongues, according to these descriptions, is not a naturally learned ability. Persons speak to God in an unknown language, one they could never have learned. Their speech sometimes is referred to as "ecstatic utterances."

For the early church, tongues offered evidence of the new reality of Christ's kingdom. In 1 Corinthians 14:22, tongues "are a sign not for believers but for unbelievers." This is why the gift of tongues is designated as a sign gift. First Corinthians 14:2 tells us that tongues speak to God and speak of the mysteries of the Spirit. As with all the gifts, tongues primarily serve to build the Christian community, the Body of Christ.

Today

Although their experiences differ, both Bill and Jim have the gift of tongues. Bill learns new second languages with ease. He is not sure why this is so. He speaks five languages. He teaches at a major university and suffers along with students who struggle to learn even the most basic structure of a new language. Bill hears a person speaking a dialect and is able to decipher enough of what the person is saying to communicate with her or him. He claims this as a gift from God, for surely he has not done anything under his own power to have this ability. Bill uses his gift in ministry with his inner-city congregation where numerous cultures and languages coexist.

Jim possesses what is referred to as "ecstatic utterances." These verbal manifestations do not correspond with any known language. He is careful in the use of his gift, because he does not want to construct linguistic barriers within the community. Instead, his gift reassures and strengthens him and others even as it praises and glorifies God. His God-given gift for speaking in tongues offers the congregation evidence that God is doing a new thing in the midst of them. His gift is understood as a sign from God, edifying the church. Jim's pastor and worshiping community accept his gift as being of God, for they see the Spirit's work in Jim as he grows in grace and as his life bears the fruit of the Spirit.

Interpretation

In the Bible

The gift of interpretation is manifested in two ways in the Bible. First, it is the special ability God gives individuals to make known what is being communicated by the person who speaks in tongues or "ecstatic utterances." In 1 Corinthians 12:10, the interpretation of tongues is listed immediately after the gift of tongues. This is for good reason. According to 1 Corinthians 14, the early church encountered a problem related to interpretation. In 1 Corinthians 14:13 and 26, Paul suggests that someone should interpret when unknown tongues are spoken so that confusion does not occur. The person with the gift of interpretation uses common speech to convey to others the message of the one who speaks in tongues—all this so that the Body of Christ, the congregation of God's people, can be uplifted.

The second use of the gift of interpretation is the ability to interpret language and meanings of words. Persons with the gift of interpretation may be linguists, who are accomplished in languages and speech forms and may utilize their gift vocationally. Specifically, they use their gift to reveal a spiritual message, thereby enhancing the growth of persons within the community. As recorded in Acts 8:26-40, the disciple Philip joined the Ethiopian in his chariot to interpret his readings. Philip served as God's instrument to lead the man to Christ.

Today

Both Philip and Mary have the gift of interpretation, although the way they express the gift differs. Philip serves in ministry with an international Bible translation group. He speaks .a number of languages fluently and deciphers dialects with little trouble. As a linguist, his lifework is to study human speech—its units, nature, structure, and modifications. Philip helps to make translations of the Scriptures available in various languages around the globe. He also has helped to write a translator's handbook on one of the Gospels, which aids translators in working to convey the total message of the gospel.

Mary's gift enables her to convey to others, in a language they understand, what is being uttered by the one who speaks in tongues. When the congregation assembles, her gift is called upon when someone speaks in tongues, as in "ecstatic utterances." Mary uses her gift to discern the message of the speaker. Sometimes Mary also speaks in tongues, interpreting her own utterances for those gathered. Mary knows her gift is an important one in the congregation. In fact, unless her gift of interpretation is present, the person with the gift of tongues may be unable to exercise his or her gift. Mary takes seriously Paul's advice in 1 Corinthians 14:13 and 26. She wants to help prevent the confusion experienced by the early church.

Gifts Versus Roles and Works of Ministry

A gift is not necessarily the same as a role or work of ministry. A gift is a specific calling upon our lives. How we live out that calling is seen in the roles and works we undertake.

You may not have the gift of giving, but as a member of Christ's church, you are called to give when the offering plate is passed and to follow the example of the widow who gave even her last pennies (Mark 12:42). You may not have the gift of evangelism, but you are commanded to witness for Jesus Christ (Matthew 28:19-20). So what's the difference?

A person with the gift places a high priority on the gift in his or her life. A person with the gift of giving may spend much time and energy raising money and distributing it to the glory of God. Those of us without the gift simply incorporate giving into our lives as one of the many ways we serve God and live out our Christian discipleship.

List below the roles and works of ministry that are high priorities in your life.

Do any of these coincide with the gifts you have identified in your life? Circle these.

Do any cause you to wonder if you may have unrecognized gifts? Underline these.

Gifts Versus Talents and Abilities

A gift is not a natural or acquired talent or ability. We all have talents and abilities and skills that we have acquired through practice or that seem to be innate. Gifts, on the other hand, can only be given to us by God.

Ms. Frye is a Sunday school teacher who makes the hour seem long and the lessons boring. Mr. Blank, on the other hand, is a teacher who gives students a passion for learning the Scriptures and excitement in their labor. It is one thing to learn the skills and proper techniques of teaching. It is an entirely different matter to possess the gift of teaching that inspires students. Ms. Frye may have acquired teaching skills, but Mr. Blank possesses the gift of teaching.

Mrs. Smith, a piano teacher, can tell you which of her students have learned the skills of playing and can get through the scales with precision. She also can enthusiastically tell you about those whose passion for music touches the very soul. Such a person's piano playing may be her or his way of using the gift of evangelism to share the gospel of Jesus Christ, or it may be her or his way of living out a specific gift, such as sharing compassion, with persons in need of God's sustaining presence. In other words, individuals use talents and abilities as expressions of God-given gifts.

Some persons appear to have a gift in the form of a talent or ability, but they are not followers of Jesus Christ. What about these persons? We believe that the Holy Spirit is at work before, during, and after a person's baptism. Even our ability to be obedient to Christ is not our work; it is God's work. We cannot take credit. The Holy Spirit, God's Spirit, is always at work in each individual, functioning to bring that person to the full knowledge of God's love through Jesus Christ. Each person we meet is of sacred worth. We need to remember that God is already at work in the people we encounter.

On the next page, list your natural or acquired talents and abilities.

How do you use these as expressions of gifts of the Spirit? Write the corresponding gift or gifts beside each talent or ability listed above.

What Will the Gift Look Like When I See It?

Reread the descriptions of your top three gifts of the Spirit as identified by the spiritual gifts survey (pages 31-35). Then list the roles, works, talents, and abilities that you see or would like to see emerging from these gifts.

EXAMPLE:
Gift of the Spirit	*Roles, Works, Talents, Abilities*
Healing	hospital chaplain; leading healing worship service; drug counseling; massage therapist; hospital visitor; supportive listening

---

Gift of the Spirit   *Roles, Works, Talents, Abilities*

1.

2.

3.

Patterns of My Life

A. List five life events or activities in which you have done something that you have found rewarding or fulfilling. These might be things you do fairly well.

1. _____

2. _____

3. _____

4. _____

5. _____

B. Find a partner. Designate one of you "talker" and the other "listener." Then spend approximately ten minutes focusing on the life events or activities listed by the talker. The talker's role is to describe the events or activities he or she has listed, sharing personal stories as appropriate. The listener's role is to use who, what, when, where, and why questions to find clarity and concrete evidence of any repeating patterns. After ten minutes, reverse roles and repeat the exercise. Note any findings below:

Discerning Our Gifts in Community

Write what you believe are your top three gifts on the lines below. Then listen for further instructions.

1. Gift: _____

Names:

2. Gift: _____

Names:

3. Gift: _____

Names:

Now sit down with one of the persons on your list and discuss why each of you thinks you have this gift. How do each of you live out the gift in concrete action? What do you have in common? What are your differences? Write what you learn from your discussion. If possible, repeat this exercise for each gift.

NOTES:

Responsive Listening Bible Study

1 C O R I N T H I A N S   1 2 : 1 2 - 2 6

The building of the community is the goal of the Spirit's work. In your small group, follow the step-by-step instructions on pages 19-20 to study 1 Corinthians 12:12-26.

> For just as the body is one and has many members, and all the members of the body, though many, are one body, so it is with Christ. For in the one Spirit we were all baptized into one body— Jews or Greeks, slaves or free—and we were all made to drink of one Spirit.
> Indeed, the body does not consist of one member but of many. If the foot would say, "Because I am not a hand, I do not belong to the body," that would not make it any less a part of the body. And if the ear would say, "Because I am not an eye, I do not belong to the body," that would not make it any less a part of the body. If the whole body were an eye, where would the hearing be? If the whole body were hearing, where would the sense of smell be? But as it is, God arranged the members in the body, each one of them, as he chose. If all were a single member, where would the body be? As it is, there are many members, yet one body. The eye cannot say to the hand, "I have no need of you," nor again the head to the feet, "I have no need of you." On the contrary, the members of the body that seem to be weaker are indispensable, and those members of the body that we think less honorable we clothe with greater honor, and our less respectable members are treated with greater respect; whereas our more respectable members do not need this. But God has so arranged the body, giving the greater honor to the inferior member, that there may be no dissension within the body, but the members may have the same care for one another. If one member suffers, all suffer together with it; if one member is honored, all rejoice together with it.

1 CORINTHIANS 12:12-26

When your group has completed the Bible study, locate and underline the gifts of the Holy Spirit named in the following passages. When you have finished, reflect on the passage in silence and wait for further instructions.

> Now concerning spiritual gifts, brothers and sisters, I do not want you to be uninformed. . . .
>
> Now there are varieties of gifts, but the same Spirit; and there are varieties of services, but the same Lord; and there are varieties of activities, but it is the same God who activates all of them in everyone. To each is given the manifestation of the Spirit for the common good. To one is given through the Spirit the utterance of wisdom, and to another the utterance of knowledge according to the same Spirit, to another faith by the same Spirit, to another gifts of healing by the one Spirit, to another the working of miracles, to another prophecy, to another the discernment of spirits, to another various kinds of tongues, to another the interpretation of tongues. All these are activated by one and the same Spirit, who allots to each one individually just as the Spirit chooses.
>
> 1 CORINTHIANS 12:1, 4-11

> Now you are the body of Christ and individually members of it. And God has appointed in the church first apostles, second prophets, third teachers; then deeds of power, then gifts of healing, forms of assistance, forms of leadership, various kinds of tongues. Are all apostles? Are all prophets? Are all teachers? Do all work miracles? Do all possess gifts of healing? Do all speak in tongues? Do all interpret? But strive for the greater gifts. And I will show you a still more excellent way.
>
> 1 CORINTHIANS 12:27-31

The Body of Christ

If you have not already done so, read and reflect on 1 Corinthians 12:12-31. Then complete this worksheet as the leader further clarifies how we are the Body of Christ.

1. _____, as a part of

_____, is the Body of Christ.

2. When the Body of Christ works as it should, it

_____ and _____.

3. We each _____ in the Body of Christ.

4. _____ comes in the Body of Christ.

5. _____ is built in the Body of Christ.

6. The congregation grows when the Body of

Christ _____

_____.

I Am a Part of the Body of Christ

Read 1 Corinthians 12:12-31.

As a part of the Body of Christ pictured here, what part are you? Color or circle it and discuss with another person why you chose this part.

Responsive Listening Bible Study

After Paul speaks extensively about the gifts of the Spirit throughout 1 Corinthians 12, he tells his readers, "But strive for the greater gifts. And I will show you a still more excellent way" (v. 31). The more excellent way that Paul refers to is the way of love.

In your small group, follow the step-by-step instructions on pages 19-20 to study the love chapter, 1 Corinthians 13.

> If I speak in the tongues of mortals and of angels, but do not have love, I am a noisy gong or a clanging cymbal. And if I have prophetic powers, and understand all mysteries and all knowledge, and if I have all faith, so as to remove mountains, but do not have love, I am nothing. If I give away all my possessions, and if I hand over my body so that I may boast, but do not have love, I gain nothing.
>
> Love is patient; love is kind; love is not envious or boastful or arrogant or rude. It does not insist on its own way; it is not irritable or resentful; it does not rejoice in wrongdoing, but rejoices in the truth. It bears all things, believes all things, hopes all things, endures all things.
>
> Love never ends. But as for prophecies, they will come to an end; as for tongues, they will cease; as for knowledge, it will come to an end. For we know only in part, and we prophesy only in part; but when the complete comes, the partial will come to an end. When I was a child, I spoke like a child, I thought like a child, I reasoned like a child; when I became an adult, I put an end to childish ways. For now we see in a mirror, dimly, but then we will see face to face. Now I know only in part; then I will know fully, even as I have been fully known. And now faith, hope, and love abide, these three; and the greatest of these is love.
>
> 1 CORINTHIANS 13

When your group has finished praying (step 8), reflect on the passage in silence and wait for further instructions.

Strive for the Greater Gifts

> But strive for the greater gifts. And I will show you a still more excellent way.
>
> 1 CORINTHIANS 12:31

Think of five people, living or dead, who have found a "still more excellent way." These are persons who center the use of their gifts in love, who know God's purpose for their lives and live in that assurance. In all that they do, they bring glory to God. Write their names and why you admire them below.

1.

2.

3.

4.

5.

For reflection: What gifts of the Spirit do you think these persons have within them? Do their gifts reflect your own gifts or others you wish to discern in yourself?

Using Our Gifts in Community

> "Let your light shine before others, so that they may see your good works and give glory to your Father in heaven."
>
> MATTHEW 5:16

1. The community invites us to _____

_____

_____.

We are the Spirit-led community of Jesus. Therefore, when we consider the tasks to be done, we should not be looking at qualifications or job slots.

2. The community helps us to_____

_____

_____.

The gifts of the Spirit enable all persons to claim ownership of the work of ministry.

3. The community stops the _____

_____

_____.

Gifts are received, not achieved. When each of us is doing the work God has called us to do, there is no hierarchy.

Responsive Listening Bible Study

ROMANS 12:3-8

Apparently the early church had members who possessed special or showy gifts and thought this made them better than others. Romans 12:3-8 is Paul's response to this attitude. In your small group, follow the step-by-step instructions on pages 19-20 to study this passage.

> For by the grace given to me I say to everyone among you not to think of yourself more highly than you ought to think, but to think with sober judgment, each according to the measure of faith that God has assigned. For as in one body we have many members, and not all the members have the same function, so we, who are many, are one body in Christ, and individually we are members one of another. We have gifts that differ according to the grace given to us: prophecy, in proportion to faith; ministry, in ministering; the teacher, in teaching; the exhorter, in exhortation; the giver, in generosity; the leader, in diligence; the compassionate, in cheerfulness.
>
> ROMANS 12:3-8

When your group has completed the Bible study, locate and underline the seven gifts named in the above passage. When you have finished, reflect on the passage in silence and wait for further instructions.

Naming One Another's Gifts

You are not journeying through SpiritGifts alone. Others are making the journey with you. With these persons you have studied the gifts of the Spirit; you have thoughtfully considered their gifts and your own; you have talked and listened to one another; you have shared stories about your past; you have talked about future dreams; you have even talked about the people who have inspired your life. You have spoken the truth to one another in love.

This exercise gives you and your fellow participants the opportunity and awesome task to identify and affirm the gifts you see evidenced in one another's lives.

WRITE YOUR NAME HERE: _____

When instructed, rise and move to write on the worksheets of three other participants. There is space to name up to three gifts for each of the three individuals you choose.

1. Writer's name: _____

   Gift(s) I see in you: _____

   _____

   _____

   Reasons I affirm this (these) gift(s):_____

   _____

   _____

   _____

   _____

2. Writer's name: _____

Gift(s) I see in you: _____

_____

_____

Reasons I affirm this (these) gift(s):_____

_____

_____

_____

_____

_____

3. Writer's name: _____

Gift(s) I see in you: _____

_____

_____

Reasons I affirm this (these) gift(s):_____

_____

_____

_____

_____

_____

A Passion for God's Purpose

List ten things that burn within you and give your life meaning. These might be the things that give you passion to live, restore your energy, and call forth the best in you. When you do these things, you feel alive and free. You know that you are living in God's will and your life has meaning.

1. _____

2. _____

3. _____

4. _____

5. _____

6. _____

7. _____

8. _____

9. _____

10. _____

What clues, if any, does this list give you about your gifts? What patterns emerge? Discuss this with a partner and with the whole group as time allows.

Responsive Listening Bible Study

MATTHEW 7:15-20; GALATIANS 5:22-25

In your small group, follow the step-by-step instructions on pages 19-20 to study these two passages that teach us about the fruit of the Spirit. Read both texts each time the instructions call for an oral reading.

"Beware of false prophets, who come to you in sheep's clothing but inwardly are ravenous wolves. You will know them by their fruits. Are grapes gathered from thorns, or figs from thistles? In the same way, every good tree bears good fruit, but the bad tree bears bad fruit. A good tree cannot bear bad fruit, nor can a bad tree bear good fruit. Every tree that does not bear good fruit is cut down and thrown into the fire. Thus you will know them by their fruits."

MATTHEW 7:15-20

By contrast, the fruit of the Spirit is love, joy, peace, patience, kindness, generosity, faithfulness, gentleness, and self-control. There is no law against such things. And those who belong to Christ Jesus have crucified the flesh with its passions and desires. If we live by the Spirit, let us also be guided by the Spirit.

GALATIANS 5:22-25

When your group has completed its study, refer back to the passage from Galatians and underline the nine fruits that are named as evidences of the Spirit's indwelling presence.

Getting Ready to Use Your Gifts

How do you get ready to use your gifts?

1. Get ready to use each gift through _____

_____.

2. Accept _____ for your gifts.

3. _____.

4. Be open to _____

_____.

Most important, share all this with God through prayer. Ask God to help you find the courage to act on what you have discerned about your gifts.

A Quick Inventory

In the column on the left, list the gifts that you have discerned and are willing to name and claim as your own. In the middle column, list the ways you are presently using each gift. In the column on the right, list concrete, tangible ways you envision yourself living out these gifts in the future.

Gift	Present Uses	Future Uses

When instructed, join others in a small group. One at a time, name one of your gifts and tell (1) how you presently use the gift and (2) what prayerful hopes and dreams you have for using the gift in the future.

A Blessed Healing

Reflect on experiences when you have found healing and whole-ness in the midst of brokenness. Remember also the times you have been blessed when you reached out to someone in a difficult season of his or her life. Think about your own healing as well as how you aided others in their need for healing. Write about these experiences in the space below.

Does your experience give you any understanding of how you might use your gifts in ministry with others? Make notes below:

Share your reflections with another person or with the group as time allows.

Responsive Listening Bible Study

ACTS   1 : 1 - 8

The book of Acts continues the narrative of Luke's Gospel by tracing the story of the Christian movement from the resurrection of Jesus to the time when the apostle Paul was preaching in Rome. Theophilus means "lover of God" and might refer to any reader who loves God. The first Christians waited in an attitude of expectant hope, and they were not disappointed.

In your small group, follow the step-by-step instructions on pages 19-20 to study Acts 1:1-8.

In the first book, Theophilus, I wrote about all that Jesus did and taught from the beginning until the day when he was taken up to heaven, after giving instructions through the Holy Spirit to the apostles whom he had chosen. After his suffering he presented himself alive to them by many convincing proofs, appearing to them during forty days and speaking about the kingdom of God. While staying with them, he ordered them not to leave Jerusalem, but to wait there for the promise of the Father. "This," he said, "is what you have heard from me; for John baptized with water, but you will be baptized with the Holy Spirit not many days from now."

So when they had come together, they asked him, "Lord, is this the time when you will restore the kingdom to Israel?" He replied, "It is not for you to know the times or periods that the Father has set by his own authority. But you will receive power when the Holy Spirit has come upon you; and you will be my witnesses in Jerusalem, in all Judea and Samaria, and to the ends of the earth."

ACTS 1:1-8

When your group has finished praying (step 8), reflect on the passage in silence and wait for further instructions.

Claiming Your Gifts for Ministry

1. List the gifts that you have named and claimed through the personal survey and study process of the SpiritGifts program.

2. List the gifts that other members of your group have affirmed in you.

3. Name the gift you feel most comfortable with and tell why.

4. Name the gift you feel least comfortable with and tell why.

5. Complete the following statement:
   These are some of the ways I may live God's will for my life using my gifts:

6. What would you like the other members of your group to remember in prayer as you continue to seek to know and live God's will for your life?

A Letter to My Congregation

Dear Friends,

I have taken part in the SpiritGifts program, along with other members of this congregation. Together we have studied, worked, and prayed to discern the gifts of the Spirit that God has given us for ministry. We understand that these gifts are not to be kept to ourselves, but are to be shared within the community, the Body of Christ. In this way we can take our needed places and live God's will and purpose for our lives.

My gifts that I have identified are:

In the past I have been involved in the following types of ministries:

In the future I would like to be involved in the following types of ministries:

_____

(Signature)

_____

(Date)

SpiritGifts Covenant and Renewal Service

Opening Song

"Many Gifts, One Spirit"

Opening Words

Prayer

Scripture

Acts 1:1-8

Reflective Comments on Scripture

From what I have heard and shared, what does God want me to do or be in this week?
How does God invite me to change?

Certificate Presentation

As you are called by name, you will be presented with a certificate of completion.

LEADER: (Name), receive this certificate as a gifted child of God.

THOSE GATHERED: (Name), we recognize God's gifts in you and pray for the Holy Spirit's guidance upon you to live God's will all the days of your life.

The Blessing

The Peace

LEADER: The peace of God, the love of Christ, and the blessings of the Holy Spirit be with you all.

THOSE GATHERED: And also with you.

LEADER: Let us share the peace with one another.

SpiritGifts Bibliography of Resources

Discover Your Gifts: A Call to Discover and Use Your Spiritual Gifts. With Chuck Bradley. Church Growth 2000, 1978. Videocassette and discussion guide. This twenty-nine-minute video is the story of a reluctant church member who discovers and uses his gifts in Christ's service. Although the clothes date the video, the humor is timeless and the teachings are solid. Available from Church Growth, Inc., P.O. Box 541, Monrovia, CA 91017.

Edwards, Lloyd. *Discerning Your Spiritual Gifts.* Cambridge, Mass.: Cowley Publications, 1988. With sound theology and reasoning, this book is a good supplementary resource for use in workshops and retreats.

Harbaugh, Gary L. *God's Gifted People: Discovering Your Personality as a Gift.* Minneapolis: Augsburg Fortress, 1990. This text is an application of the Myers-Briggs Personality Type Indicator, the most widely used measure of personalities, dispositions, and preferences. It combines the gifts of the Spirit with psychological insights to search out reflections on faith and daily life.

Hawkins, Thomas R. *Claiming God's Promises: A Guide to Discovering Your Spiritual Gifts.* Nashville: Abingdon Press, 1992. This book includes a process for individuals as well as groups to progress toward a deeper spiritual life and broader ministry. The author explores biblical passages related to the gift of ministry.

Kinghorn, Kenneth Cain. *Gifts of the Spirit.* Nashville: Abingdon Press, 1976. Kinghorn offers insights and advice about how to accept and use the gifts of God. The book goes beyond instruction to inspire, sharpen understanding, and stimulate commitment.

Page, Patricia N. *All God's People Are Ministers: Equipping Church Members for Ministry.* Minneapolis: Augsburg Fortress, 1993. The primary goal of this book is to strengthen laypeople in their ministry. It shows how the people of God can be helped to discover how important their ministry is and how they can be empowered to carry out their ministry.

Schmitt, Harley H. *Many Gifts, One Lord: A Biblical Understanding of the Variety of Spiritual Gifts Among the Early Christians and in the Church Today.* Minneapolis: Augsburg Fortress, 1993. An excellent scholarly resource that walks the reader through the New Testament passages pertaining to the gifts of the Spirit. The author then applies the gifts to contemporary life.

Notes

Notes

Notes

Notes

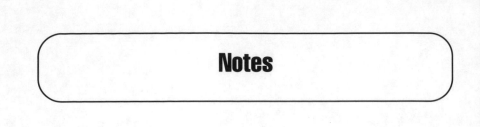

Notes

Notes

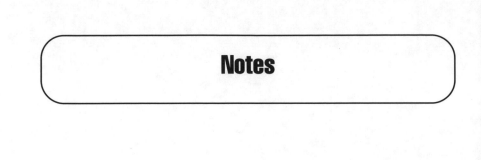

Notes